WiSDOM

THE GREATEST THINGS EVER SAID

WiSDOM

Leonard Roy Frank

RANDOM HOUSE
REFERENCE

INTRODUCTION

*W*hatever happened to wisdom? Somehow it's been lost in the shuffle of modern life. We're stuffed with knowledge and starved for wisdom. As T. S. Eliot wrote—before the advent of the computer age—"Where is the wisdom we have lost in knowledge? Where is the knowledge we have lost in information?" What would he think were he alive today?

But this book is not so much about wisdom per se as it is about the world's wisdom. Gathered here are more than 270 of what I consider to be the wisest, smartest things ever said. These have been culled from forty years of reading and study. In making the selections, I've used the following criteria: simplicity (all the quotations are understandable independent of context), brevity (no quotation is longer than a sentence), universality (they are truths on *both* sides of the Pyrenees), and usefulness (they are intended to be helpful in making sense of ourselves and our world and/or providing guidelines for living). A compilation such as this is by its very nature highly subjective; the end product is, for better or worse, a belief system, a personal credo.

THE NEW WISDOM WHICH THE NEW WORLD REQUIRES will be learned sooner or later; . . . the best part of human history lies in the future, not in the past.

Bertrand Russell, English mathematician and philosopher, 1872–1970

YOU NEVER REALLY understand a person until you consider things from his point of view—until you climb into his skin and walk around in it.

Harper Lee, contemporary U.S. writer (in the novel To Kill a Mockingbird, *1960)*

IT MAY BE THAT THE WHOLE IS SIMPLE, AND THAT WE ARE LOOKING AT IT FROM THE WRONG POINT OF VIEW.

Henri Bergson, French philosopher, 1859–1941 (in The Two Sources of Morality and Religion, *1932)*

*L*ife is short, the art long, opportunity fleeting, experience treacherous, judgment difficult.

Hippocrates, Greek physician, fifth century B.C.

*L*ife is what happens to you while you're busy making other plans.

John Lennon, English songwriter and singer, 1940–1980
(in the song "Beautiful Boy," 1981)

KNOWLEDGE, love, power—there is the complete life.

Henri Amiel, Swiss poet and philosopher, 1821–1881

The unexamined life is not worth living.

Socrates, Greek philosopher, fifth century B.C.

I am a human being; nothing human is alien to me.

Terence, Roman playwright, second century B.C.

I think, therefore I am.

René Descartes, French philosopher, 1596–1650

I think that Man is immortal, but not men.

H. G. Wells, English writer and historian, 1866–1946

7

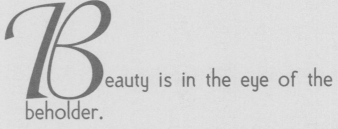

Beauty is in the eye of the beholder.

Margaret Wolfe Hungerford, Irish writer, 1855–1897

We see things as we are, not as they are.

Jennifer Stone, contemporary U.S. writer

ONE half the troubles of this life can be traced to saying "yes" too quick, and not saying "no" soon enough.

Josh Billings, U.S. writer and humorist, 1818–1885

We are the choices we have made.

Meryl Streep, contemporary U.S. actor

The function of art is to do more than tell it like it is—*it's to imagine what is possible.*

bell hooks, contemporary U.S. poet and writer

THERE IS AS MUCH DIGNITY IN TILLING A FIELD AS IN WRITING A POEM.

Booker T. Washington, U.S. educator and writer, 1856–1915

Give me a lever long enough and a fulcrum strong enough, and single-handedly I will move the world.

Archimedes, Greek scientist, third century B.C.

To every action there is always opposed an equal reaction.

Isaac Newton, English physicist, 1642–1727

THE INTERPRETATION OF DREAMS

is the via regia [royal road] to a knowledge of the uncon-scious element in our psychic life.

Sigmund Freud, Austrian physician and founder of psychoanalysis, 1856–1939 (in The Interpretation of Dreams, *1900)*

14

I have called this principle, by which each slight variation, if useful, is preserved, by the term of Natural Selection.
Charles Darwin, English naturalist, 1809–1882 (in On the Origin of the Species, *1859)*

$$E = mc^2$$

(energy equals mass times the speed of light squared)
Albert Einstein, German-born U.S. physicist, 1879–1955

What we have to learn to do, we learn by doing.

Aristotle, Greek philosopher, fourth century B.C.

PRACTICE MAKES PERFECT.

English Proverb

Unlearning is more difficult than learning.

English Proverb

NOTHING HAS MORE retarded the advancement of learning than the disposition of vulgar minds to ridicule and vilify what they cannot comprehend.

Samuel Johnson, English writer and lexicographer, 1709–1784

Much learning does not teach understanding.

Heraclitus, Greek philosopher, fifth century B.C.

An ounce of common sense is worth a pound of learning.

Persian Proverb

17

Children have more need of models than of critics.

Joseph Joubert, French moralist, 1754–1824

I educate, not by lessons, but by going about my business.

Socrates, Greek philosopher, fifth century B.C.

He does not educate children but rejoices in their happiness.

Herman Hesse, German writer, 1877–1962

*T*HE true university of these days is a collection of books.

Thomas Carlyle, English historian, 1775–1881

'Tis education forms the common mind,
Just as the twig is bent, the tree's inclined.

Alexander Pope, English poet, 1688–1744
(in the poem "Moral Essays," 1731–1735)

Education has for its object the formation of character.

Herbert Spencer, English philosopher, 1820–1903

Example is the best precept.

Aesop, Greek storyteller, sixth century B.C.

SUCH is the irresistible nature of truth that all it asks, and all it wants, is the liberty of appearing.

Thomas Paine, English-born U.S. political philosopher, 1737–1809

We are not afraid to follow truth wherever it may lead, nor to tolerate any error so long as reason is left free to combat it.

Thomas Jefferson, U.S. president, 1743–1826

UNSPOKEN TRUTHS BECOME POISONOUS.

Friedrich Nietzsche, German philosopher, 1844–1900

When we have arrived at the question, the answer is already near.

Ralph Waldo Emerson, U.S. philosopher, 1803–1882

The simplest and most necessary truths are always the last believed.

John Ruskin, English art critic and writer, 1819–1900

TRUTH, [THAT] OPPOSETH no man's profit, nor pleasure, is to all men welcome.

Thomas Hobbes, English philosopher, 1588–1679
(closing sentence of Leviathan, *1651)*

Truth angers those it does not convince.

Anonymous

The weakness of a soul is proportionate to the number of truths which must be kept from it.

Eric Hoffer, U.S. longshoreman and writer, 1902–1983
(in The Passionate State of Mind, *1954)*

24

WHAT plays the devil in human affairs is mistaking a half-truth for a whole truth.

Alfred North Whitehead, English mathematician and philosopher,
1861–1947

Truth is always subversive.

Anne Lamott, contemporary U.S. writer

The truth knocks on the door and you say, "Go away, I'm looking for the truth," and so it goes away. Puzzling.

Robert M. Pirsig, contemporary U.S. writer (in Zen and the Art of Motorcycle Maintenance: An Inquiry into Values, *1974)*

Not even the most devastating truth can be told; it must be evoked.

Joyce Carol Oates, contemporary U.S. writer

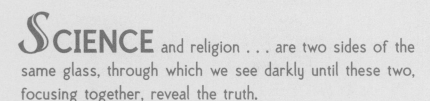

SCIENCE and religion . . . are two sides of the same glass, through which we see darkly until these two, focusing together, reveal the truth.

Pearl S. Buck, U.S. writer, 1892–1973

All religions, arts and sciences are branches of the same tree.

Albert Einstein, German-born U.S. physicist, 1879–1955

KNOWLEDGE . . . IS POWER.

Francis Bacon, English philosopher, 1561–1626

To know what you know and to know what you do not know—*that is knowledge.*

Confucius, Chinese founder of Confucianism, sixth century B.C.
(in Confucian Analects*)*

Every great advance in natural knowledge has involved the absolute rejection of authority.

T. H. Huxley, English biologist, 1825–1895

*F*IGURING out who you are is the whole point of the human experience.

Anna Quindlen, contemporary U.S. journalist

Know thyself.

Thales, Greek philosopher, sixth century B.C.

If self-knowledge is the road to virtue, so is virtue still more the road to self-knowledge.

Jean Paul Friedrich Richter, German writer, 1763–1825

LET US HAVE FAITH THAT RIGHT MAKES MIGHT, AND IN THAT FAITH, LET US, TO THE END, DARE TO DO OUR DUTY AS WE UNDERSTAND IT.

Abraham Lincoln, U.S. president, 1809–1865 (1860)

'Tis not in mortals to command success,
But we'll do more, Sempronius; we'll deserve it.

Joseph Addison, English writer, 1672–1719 (in the play Cato, *1713)*

'Tis not the dying for a faith that is so hard, Master Harry—'tis the living up to it that is difficult.

William Makepeace Thackeray, English writer, 1811–1863 (in the novel The History of Henry Esmond, *1852)*

*J*ust as virtue is its own reward,
so is vice its own punishment.

Baltasar Gracián, Spanish writer, 1601–1658
(in The Art of Worldly Wisdom, *1647)*

M

oderation in temper is always a virtue, but moderation in principle is a species of vice.

Thomas Paine, English-born U.S. political philosopher,
1737–1809

SOCIETY can only be happy and free in proportion as it is virtuous.

Mary Wollstonecraft, English writer, 1759–1797
(in A Vindication of the Rights of Woman, *1792)*

Human service is the highest form of self-interest.

Elbert Hubbard, U.S. writer, editor, and humorist, 1856–1915

THE HIGHEST WISDOM IS KINDNESS.

Talmud, ancient Hebrew religious writing

Wise late, old soon; wise soon, old late.

English Proverb

The wise learn from the mistakes of others; fools, not even from their own.

English Proverb

The invariable mark of wisdom is to see the miraculous in the common.

Ralph Waldo Emerson, U.S. philosopher, 1803–1882

*W*isdom consists of the anticipation of consequences.

Norman Cousins, U.S. editor and writer, 1915–1990

ONE who lives according to the Way is one who embodies wisdom and compassion.

Amaro Bhikkhu, contemporary Buddhist monk

In this world, you must be a bit too kind in order to be kind enough.

Pierre Marivaux, French playwright, 1688–1763

Right belief; right intentions; right speech; right actions; right liveli-
hood; right endeavoring; right mindfulness; right concentration.

The Buddha, Nepalese founder of Buddhism, sixth century B.C.

Treasures gained by wickedness do not profit.

Bible (Proverbs 10:2)

DO UNTO OTHERS AS YOU WOULD HAVE THEM DO UNTO YOU.

Jesus, Hebrew founder of Christianity, first century A.D. (Matthew 7:12)

GIVE AS YOU WOULD RECEIVE.

English Proverb

As the body apart from the spirit is dead, so faith apart from works is dead.

James, Christian apostle, first century A.D. (James 2:26)

There lives more faith in honest doubt,
Believe me, than in half the creeds.

Alfred, Lord Tennyson, English poet, 1809–1892

42

NEVER GOOD THROUGH EVIL.

Proverb

By doing good we become good.
Jean-Jacques Rousseau, French philosopher, 1712–1778
(in Emile; or, Treatise on Education, *1762)*

The meaning of good and bad . . . is simply helping or hurting.
Ralph Waldo Emerson, U.S. philosopher, 1803–1882

43

The moral sentiment . . . is the drop
that balances the sea.

Ralph Waldo Emerson, U.S. philosopher, 1803–1882
(in Representative Men, 1850)

There is only one morality . . . just as there is only one geometry.

𝒯HERE is a measure of free will within a system of predestination.

Aldous Huxley, English writer, 1894–1963

Without freedom there can be no morality.

Carl G. Jung, Swiss psychiatrist and founder of analytical psychology, 1875–1961

FOOD FIRST, THEN ETHICS.

Bertolt Brecht, German playwright, 1898–1956 (in the play The Threepenny Opera, *1928)*

Ethics is reverence for *all* life.

Albert Schweitzer, German physician and theologian, 1875–1965 (in the essay "Religion and Modern Civilization," 1934)

THE HIGHEST MORAL LAW IS THAT WE SHOULD UNREMITTINGLY WORK FOR THE GOOD OF MANKIND.

Mohandas K. Gandhi, Indian spiritual and nationalist leader, 1869–1948

THE ONLY WISE AND SAFE COURSE is to act from day to day in accordance with what one's own conscience seems to decree.

Winston Churchill, British prime minister, 1874–1965
(in The Second World War: The Gathering Storm, *1948)*

THERE IS ONLY ONE CATEGORICAL IMPERATIVE: Act only according to that maxim by which you can at the same time will that it should become a universal law.

Immanuel Kant, German philosopher, 1724–1804
(in Foundations of the Metaphysics of Morals, *1797)*

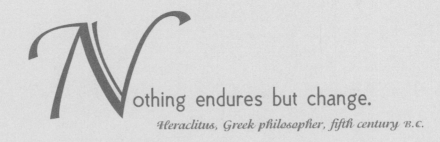

Nothing endures but change.

Heraclitus, Greek philosopher, fifth century B.C.

The human species is forever in a state of change, forever becoming.

Simone de Beauvoir, French writer, 1908–1986

IN a nation of millions and a world of billions, the individual is still the first and basic agent of change.

Lyndon B. Johnson, U.S. president, 1908–1973

A capacity to change is indispensable. Equally indispensable is the capacity to hold fast to that which *is good*.

John Foster Dulles, U.S. secretary of state, 1888–1959

ALL THAT IS HUMAN must retrograde if it [does] not advance.

Edward Gibbon, English historian, 1737–1794 (in The Decline and Fall of the Roman Empire, *1776–1788)*

The free intellect is the chief engine of human progress.

Bertrand Russell, English mathematician and philosopher, 1872–1970

The world hangs on a thin thread, and that thread is the psyche of man.

Carl G. Jung, Swiss psychiatrist and founder of analytical psychology, 1875–1961 (in Two Essays on Analytical Psychology, *1953)*

THE kicking is hardest just before the birth.

Proverb

Ripeness is all.

William Shakespeare, English playwright, 1564–1616 (in the play King Lear, *1605)*

THE ABSOLUTE IMPOSSIBILITY of the continuance of the state in its present condition must become the universal conviction before things can become in any way better.

Albert Schweitzer, German physician and theologian, 1875–1965

HOW SOCIETY WAITS UNFORMED, AND IS FOR A WHILE BETWEEN THINGS ENDED AND THINGS BEGUN.

Walt Whitman, U.S. poet, 1819–1891

CHANGE occurs when there is a confluence of both changing values and economic necessity, not before.

John Naisbitt, contemporary U.S. futurist

Sometimes it takes the vision of disaster to bring nations to their senses.

James Reston, U.S. journalist, 1909–1995

Without opposition, no progress.

Karl Marx, German economist and philosopher, 1818–1883

Discontent is the first necessity of progress.

Thomas Alva Edison, U.S. inventor, 1847–1931

Necessity is the mother of invention.

Plato, Greek philosopher, fourth century B.C.

NECESSITY HAS NO LAW.

St. Augustine, Christian theologian, fourth century A.D.

𝒯HOSE who cannot remember the past are con-
demned to repeat it.

George Santayana, Spanish-born U.S. philosopher, 1863–1952
(in The Life of Reason, *1906)*

We read the world wrong and say that it *deceives*
us.

Rabindranath Tagore, Indian philosopher, 1861–1941

HUMAN HISTORY BECOMES MORE AND MORE A RACE BETWEEN EDUCATION AND CATASTROPHE.

H. G. Wells, English writer and historian, 1866–1946
(in The Outline of History, *1920)*

HISTORY TEACHES US that men and nations behave wisely once they have exhausted all other alternatives.

Abba Eban, South African–born Israeli diplomat, 1915–2002

The present may be as much determined by the future as by the past.

Lewis Mumford, U.S. sociologist, 1895–1990
(in The Conduct of Life, *1951)*

There seems no plan because it is all plan.

C. S. Lewis, English writer, 1898–1963

*T*URN where we may, within, around, the voice of great events is proclaiming to us, "Reform, that you may preserve."

Thomas Babington Macaulay, English writer and member of Parliament, 1800–1859 (House of Commons speech, March 2, 1831)

Those who make peaceful revolution impossible will make violent revolution inevitable.

John F. Kennedy, U.S. president, 1917–1962

IF A NATION expects to be ignorant and free, it expects what never was and never will be.

Thomas Jefferson, U.S. president, 1743–1826

An immoral nation invites its own ruin.

Dwight D. Eisenhower, U.S. president, 1890–1969

THE RUIN OF A NATION BEGINS IN THE HOMES OF ITS PEOPLE.

Ashanti Proverb

Force and fraud are in war with the two cardinal virtues.
Thomas Hobbes, English philosopher, 1588–1679

War is a continuation of politics by other means.
Karl von Clausewitz, German military theorist, 1780–1831
(in On War, 1832)

WAR IS HELL.
William Tecumseh Sherman, U.S. general, 1820–1891(1879)

THERE IS NO NATION ON EARTH SO DANGEROUS AS A NATION FULLY ARMED, AND BANKRUPT AT HOME.

Henry Cabot Lodge, Massachusetts senator, 1850–1924

In the councils of government, we must guard against the acquisition of unwarranted influence, whether sought or unsought, by the military-industrial complex.

Dwight D. Eisenhower, U.S. president, 1890–1969
(Farewell Address, January 17, 1961)

What we now need to discover in the social realm is the moral equivalent of war: something heroic that will speak to men as universally as war does, and yet will be as compatible with their spiritual selves as war has proven itself to be incompatible.

William James, U.S. physician, psychologist, and philosopher, 1842–1910 (in The Varieties of Religious Experience: A Study in Human Nature, *1902)*

TODAY THE CHOICE IS NO LONGER BETWEEN VIOLENCE AND NONVIOLENCE; IT IS EITHER NONVIOLENCE OR NONEXISTENCE.

Martin Luther King Jr., U.S. clergyman and human rights leader, 1929–1968 (in Stride Toward Freedom, *1958)*

THE hottest places in hell are reserved for those who in a time of great moral crisis maintain their neutrality.

Dante Alighieri, Italian poet, 1265–1321

The only thing necessary for evil to triumph is for good men to do nothing.

Edmund Burke, English statesman and philosopher, 1729–1797
(attributed)

*N*othing is more powerful than an idea whose time has come.

Victor Hugo, French writer, 1802–1885
(in the novel Histoire d'un crime, *1877)*

Ideas won't keep. Something must be done about them.

Alfred North Whitehead, English mathematician and philosopher, 1861–1947 (in Dialogues, 1954)

As life is action and passion,

it is required of a man that he should share the passion and action of his time at peril of being judged not to have lived.

Oliver Wendell Holmes Jr., U.S. Supreme Court chief justice, 1841–1935

In our era, the road to holiness necessarily passes through the world of action.

Dag Hammarskjöld, Swedish statesman and UN secretary general, 1905–1961 (in Markings, 1964)

72

CHARACTER IS DESTINY.

Heraclitus, Greek philosopher, fifth century B.C.

Self-trust is the essence of heroism.

Ralph Waldo Emerson, U.S. philosopher, 1803–1882

Self-esteem isn't everything; it's just that there's nothing without it.

Gloria Steinem, contemporary U.S. women's rights leader and writer
(in Revolution from Within, 1992)

73

COURAGE IS RIGHTLY ESTEEMED THE FIRST OF HUMAN QUALITIES BECAUSE . . . IT IS THE QUALITY WHICH GUARANTEES ALL OTHERS.

Winston Churchill, British prime minister, 1874–1965
(in Great Contemporaries, *1937)*

CHANCE favors only the prepared mind.
Louis Pasteur, French chemist, 1822–1895

Fortune favors the brave.
Terence, Roman playwright, second century B.C.

NEXT to knowing when to seize an opportunity, the most important thing in life is to know when to forego an advantage.

Benjamin Disraeli, English prime minister, 1804–1881

Whether you believe you can do a thing or not, you are right.

Henry Ford, U.S. industrialist, 1863–1947

THE PEOPLE WHO GET ON in this world are the people who get up and look for the circumstances they want, and, if they don't find them, make them.

George Bernard Shaw, British playwright and critic, 1856–1950
(in the play Mrs. Warren's Profession, *1893)*

THE WINDS AND THE WAVES ARE ALWAYS ON THE SIDE OF THE ABLEST NAVIGATORS.

Edward Gibbon, English historian, 1737–1794

77

WHEN A TRUE genius appears in the world, you may know him by this sign, that the dunces are all in confederacy against him.
Jonathan Swift, English clergyman and writer, 1667–1745

The secret of genius is . . . *to honor every truth by use.*
Ralph Waldo Emerson, U.S. philosopher, 1803–1882
(in Representative Men, *1850)*

Genius is one percent inspiration and ninety-nine percent perspiration.
Thomas Alva Edison, U.S. inventor, 1847–1931

LAWS ARE LIKE cobwebs that entangle the weak but are broken by the strong.

Anacharsis, Scythian prince and philosopher, sixth century B.C.

People say law but they mean wealth.

Ralph Waldo Emerson, U.S. philosopher, 1803–1882

THE MORE LAWS, THE LESS JUSTICE.

German Proverb

*J*USTICE is truth in action.

Joseph Joubert, French moralist, 1754–1824

Let justice roll down like waters,
and righteousness like an ever-flowing stream.

Amos, Hebrew prophet, eighth century B.C. (Amos 5:24)

THE FUNDAMENTAL CONFLICTS in

human life are not between competing ideas—one of which is true and the other false, but rather, between those that hold power and use it to oppress others, and those who are oppressed by power and seek to free themselves of it.

Thomas S. Szasz, contemporary Hungarian-born U.S. psychiatrist

The lust for power is not rooted in strength but in weakness.

Erich Fromm, German-born U.S. psychoanalyst, 1900–1980

*T*he vision of a world community based on justice, not power, is the necessity of our age.

Henry A. Kissinger, German-born U.S. secretary of state
(in Years of Upheaval, *1982)*

There can be no justice without peace and there can be no peace without justice.

$\mathcal{A}$LL government without the consent of the governed is the very definition of slavery.

Jonathan Swift, English clergyman and writer, 1667–1745

Let the people think they govern, and they will be governed.

William Penn, English-born Pennsylvania governor and religious leader, 1644–1718 (in Some Fruits of Solitude, *1693)*

WITH FAMILY GOVERNMENTS, as with political ones, a harsh despotism itself generates a great part of the crimes it has to repress.

Herbert Spencer, English philosopher, 1820–1903
(in Education: Intellectual, Moral, and Physical, *1860)*

THE BEST GOVERNMENT IS THAT WHICH GOVERNS LEAST.

John L. O'Sullivan, U.S. writer, 1813–1895

A government which robs Peter to pay Paul can always depend on the support of Paul.

George Bernard Shaw, British playwright and critic, 1856–1950

The technique of acquiring dictator-
ship over what has been a democracy
always involves a mixture of bribery,
propaganda and violence.

Bertrand Russell, English mathematician and philosopher,
1872–1970 (in Power: A New Social Analysis, *1938)*

Of all the tyrannies on humankind,
The worst is that which persecutes
the mind.

John Dryden, English poet, 1631–1700
(in the poem "The Hind and the Panther",
1687)

POLITICAL language . . . is designed to make lies sound truthful and murder respectable, and to give the appearance of solidity to pure wind.

George Orwell, English writer, 1903–1950 (in the essay "Politics and the English Language," 1946)

Cunning and treachery indicate lack of skill.

François de La Rochefoucauld, French writer, 1613–1680

CAUGHT IN ONE LIE, ALWAYS SUSPECT.

Proverb

~

The punishment of the liar is that he eventually believes his own lies.

Elbert Hubbard, U.S. writer, editor, and humorist, 1856–1915

~

Lying is done with words, and also with silence.

Adrienne Rich, contemporary U.S. poet and writer (in the essay "Women and Honor: Some Notes on Lying," 1975)

LIBERTY CONSISTS IN being able to do anything that doesn't harm others.

The Declaration of the Rights of Man and the Citizen, *1789*

Those who would give up essential liberty to purchase a little temporary safety deserve neither liberty nor safety.

Benjamin Franklin, U.S. printer, inventor, and statesman, 1706–1790

Eternal vigilance is the price of liberty.

Wendell Phillips, U.S. abolitionist and social reformer, 1811–1884

ECONOMIC FREEDOM CANNOT be
sacrificed if political freedom is to be preserved.

Herbert Hoover, U.S. president, 1874–1964

There are more instances of the abridgment of the freedom of the people by gradual and silent encroachments of those in power than by violent and sudden usurpations.

James Madison, U.S. president, 1751–1836

THE GREATEST DANGERS to liberty lurk in insidious encroachment by men of zeal, well-meaning but without understanding.

Louis D. Brandeis, U.S. Supreme Court associate justice, 1856–1941

Most of the greatest evils that man has inflicted upon man have come through people feeling quite certain about something which, in fact, *was false.*

Bertrand Russell, English mathematician and philosopher,
1872–1970

THE RIGHT TO BE LET ALONE—

the most comprehensive of rights and the right most valued by civilized men.

Louis D. Brandeis, U.S. Supreme Court associate justice, 1856–1941

LIBERTY LIES IN THE HEARTS OF MEN AND WOMEN; WHEN IT DIES THERE, NO CONSTITUTION, NO LAW, NO COURT CAN SAVE IT.

Learned Hand, U.S. jurist, 1872–1961

RIGHTS that do not flow directly from duty well performed are not worth having.

Mohandas K. Gandhi, Indian spiritual and nationalist leader,
1869–1948

Liberty and responsibility are inseparable.

F. A. Hayek, Austrian-born English economist and philosopher,
1899–1992

If men and women are in chains anywhere in the world, then freedom is endangered everywhere.

John F. Kennedy, U.S. president, 1917–1962

*N*obody's free until everybody's free.

Fannie Lou Hamer, U.S. human rights leader, 1917–1977

WHEN I DO good, I feel good. When I do bad, I feel bad. That's my religion.

Anonymous U.S. clergyman (as recalled by Abraham Lincoln in 1865)

My country is the world, and my religion is to do good.

Thomas Paine, English-born U.S. political philosopher, 1737–1809

Our country, right or wrong; if right, to be kept right; and if wrong, *to be set right!*

Carl Schurz, German-born Missouri senator and journalist, 1829–1906

Always think of the universe as one living organism, with a single substance and a single soul.

Marcus Aurelius, Roman emperor and philosopher, second century A.D. (in Meditations*)*

I do not believe there are two separate worlds, the spiritual and the material. They are two aspects of one and the same universe.

André Gide, French writer, 1869–1951

THE UNIVERSE IS MADE OF STORIES
NOT OF ATOMS.

Muriel Rukeyser, U.S. poet and writer, 1913–1980 (in the poem "The Speed of Darkness," 1968)

THE RIVER IS WITHIN US, THE SEA IS ALL ABOUT US.

T. S. Eliot, U.S.-born English poet, 1888–1965 (in the poem "The Dry Salvages," 1943)

IT IS NOT enough for me to ask questions; I want to know how to answer the one question that seems to encompass everything: *What am I here for?*

Abraham Joshua Heschel, German-born U.S. theologian, 1907–1972 (in Who Is Man? *1965)*

100

THE MOST IMPORTANT LESSON I

learned [as a prisoner of war] was that to sustain my self-respect for a lifetime it would be necessary for me to have the honor of serving something greater than my self-interest.

John McCain, contemporary Arizona senator

AS SURELY AS WE ARE DRIVEN TO LIVE, WE ARE DRIVEN TO SERVE SPIRITUAL ENDS THAT SURPASS OUR OWN INTERESTS.

Abraham Joshua Heschel, German-born U.S. theologian, 1907–1972

ENLARGED MATERIAL POWERS SPELL ENLARGED
PERIL IF THERE IS NOT PROPORTIONATE GROWTH
OF THE SOUL.

*Martin Luther King Jr., U.S. clergyman and human rights leader,
1929–1968 (in* Where Do We Go from Here:
Chaos or Community?, *1967)*

FACTS do not cease to exist because they are ignored.

Aldous Huxley, English writer, 1894–1963

If way to the Better there be, it exacts a full look at the Worst.

Thomas Hardy, English writer and poet, 1840–1928

To transform the world and society, we must first and foremost transform ourselves.

Ho Chi Minh, Vietnamese president, 1890–1969

He not busy bein' born is busy dyin'.

*Bob Dylan, contemporary U.S. songwriter and singer
(in the song "It's Alright, Ma (I'm Only Bleeding)," 1965)*

NO GREAT IMPROVEMENTS in the lot of mankind are possible until a great change takes place in the fundamental constitution of their modes of thought.

John Stuart Mill, English philosopher, 1806–1873

The greatest need in the world at this moment is the transformation of *human nature.*

Billy Graham, contemporary U.S. evangelist

WE are not going in circles, we are going upwards.
The path is spiral.

Herman Hesse, German writer, 1877–1962
(in the novel Siddhartha, *1922)*

A man differs from a microbe only in being
further on the path.

George Bernard Shaw, British playwright and critic, 1856–1950
(in the play Back to Methuselah, *1921)*

THE PROCESS OF EVOLUTION can only be described as the gradual insertion of more and more freedom into matter.

T. E. Hulme, English philosopher, 1883–1917

IF WE TAKE PEOPLE ONLY AS THEY ARE, WE MAKE THEM WORSE; if we treat them as though they were what they ought to be, we steer them in the right direction.

Johann Wolfgang von Goethe, German poet and writer, 1749–1832

IF YOU'RE COMING TO HELP ME,

you are wasting your time. But if you have come because your liberation is bound up with mine, then let us work together.

Anonymous Aboriginal Australian woman (quoted in Jim Wallis, The Soul of Politics: A Practical and Prophetic Vision for Change, *1994)*

Only those who have helped themselves know how to help others, and *to respect their right to help themselves.*

George Bernard Shaw, British playwright and critic, 1856–1950

MORAL RESPONSIBILITY IS NOT just a matter of avoiding harm to others; it also means helping people in need.

Michael Nedelsky, contemporary U.S. clergyman

God helps those who help themselves; God help those who don't.

Anonymous

No bird soars too high, if he soars with his own wings.

William Blake, English poet and artist, 1757–1827

IF A MAN write a better book, preach a better sermon, or make a better mousetrap than his neighbor, though he build his house in the woods, the world will make a beaten path to his door.

Ralph Waldo Emerson, U.S. philosopher, 1803–1882

EVERYTHING THAT MATTERS IN OUR INTELLECTUAL AND MORAL LIFE BEGINS WITH AN INDIVIDUAL CONFRONTING HIS OWN MIND AND CONSCIENCE IN A ROOM BY HIMSELF.

Arthur M. Schlesinger Jr., contemporary U.S. historian (in the essay "The Decline of Greatness," 1958)

111

If a man does not keep pace with his companions, perhaps it is because he hears a different drummer. Let him step to the music that he hears, however measured or far away.

Henry David Thoreau, U.S. philosopher, 1817–1862
(in Walden; or Life in the Woods, 1854)

For nonconformity the world whips you with its displeasure. And therefore a man must know how to estimate a sour face.

Ralph Waldo Emerson, U.S. philosopher, 1803–1882
(in the essay "Self-Reliance," 1841)

IN the beginning God created the heavens and the earth.

Bible (Genesis 1:1)

God is one.

Moses, Hebrew founder of Judaism, fourteenth century B.C.
(Deuteronomy 6:4)

GOD IS A CIRCLE WHOSE CENTER IS EVERY-
WHERE AND CIRCUMFERENCE NOWHERE.

Timaeus of Locris, Greek astronomer, fourth century B.C.

DO NOT BE DECEIVED; God is not mocked,
for whatever a man sows, that he will also reap.

Paul, Christian apostle, first century A.D. (Galatians 6:7)

I FORM THE LIGHT, AND CREATE DARKNESS; I make peace, and create evil; I am the Lord, that doeth all these things.

Isaiah, Hebrew prophet, eighth century B.C. (Isaiah 45:7, Masoretic text)

HE HAS SHOWED YOU, O MAN, WHAT IS GOOD; and what does the Lord require of you but to do justice, and to love kindness, and to walk humbly with your God.

Micah, Hebrew prophet, eighth century B.C. (Micah 6:8)

117

Where the Spirit of the Lord is present, there is freedom.

Paul, Christian apostle, first century A.D. (2 Corinthians 3:17)

Do you love your Creator? Love your fellow-beings first.

Muhammad, Arab founder of Islam, 570–632 A.D.

If God is, whence come evil things? If He is not, whence come good?

Boethius, Roman philosopher, sixth century A.D.

WE have forgotten the age-old fact that God speaks chiefly through dreams and visions.

Carl G. Jung, Swiss psychiatrist and founder of analytical psychology, 1875–1961 (in the essay "Approaching the Unconscious," 1964)

God is conscience.

Mohandas K. Gandhi, Indian spiritual and nationalist leader, 1869–1948

To err is human; to forgive, divine.

*Alexander Pope, English poet, 1688–1744
(in the poem "An Essay on Criticism," 1711)*

To understand is not only to pardon,
but in the end to love.

Walter Lippmann, U.S. journalist, 1889–1974
(in A Preface to Morals, 1929)

*T*HE meaning of life consists in the love and service of God.

Leo Tolstoy, Russian writer, 1828–1910 (in The Kingdom of God Is Within You, *1893)*

Man's extremity is God's opportunity.

English Proverb

What is most needed is a loving heart.
The Buddha, Nepalese founder of Buddhism, sixth century B.C.

THE WORST SIN TOWARDS OUR FELLOW CREATURES
IS NOT TO HATE THEM, BUT TO BE INDIFFERENT
TO THEM: THAT'S THE ESSENCE OF INHUMANITY.
George Bernard Shaw, British playwright and critic, 1856–1950

*T*HE real problem of our existence lies in the fact that we ought to love one another, but do not.

Reinhold Niebuhr, U.S. theologian, 1892–1971

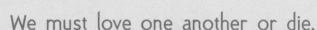

We must love one another or die.

W. H. Auden, English-born U.S. poet, 1907–1973 (in the poem "September 1, 1939," 1940)

THERE IS NO true intimacy between souls who do not know how to respect one another's solitude.

Thomas Merton, U.S. monk and writer, 1915–1968 (in No Man Is an Island, *1955)*

Mutual love, the crown of all our bliss.

John Milton, English poet, 1608–1674 (in the poem "Paradise Lost", 1667)

Families break up when people take hints you don't intend and miss hints you do intend.

Robert Frost, U.S. poet, 1874–1963

125

By mutual confidence and mutual aid
Great deeds are done, and great
discoveries made.

Alexander Pope, English poet, 1688–1744

FRIENDSHIP MAY WELL deserve the sacrifice of pleasure, though not of conscience.

Samuel Johnson, English writer and lexicographer, 1709–1784

Friends share all things.

Pythagoras, Greek philosopher, sixth century B.C.

SHARED JOYS ARE DOUBLED; SHARED SORROWS ARE HALVED.

English Proverb

As to diseases, make a habit of two things: to help, or at least, do no harm.

Hippocrates, Greek physician, fifth century B.C.
(in the "Hippocratic Oath")

*T*he best doctors in the world are Doctor Diet, Doctor Quiet and Doctor Merryman.

Jonathan Swift, English writer, 1667–1745

MANY dishes, many diseases; many medicines, few cures.

Benjamin Franklin, U.S. printer, inventor, and statesman, 1706–1790

An ounce of prevention is worth *a pound of cure.*

English Proverb

HE WHO DOES NOT understand your silence will probably not understand your words.

Elbert Hubbard, U.S. writer, editor, and humorist, 1856–1915

Speech is of time, silence is of eternity.

Thomas Carlyle, English historian, 1775–1881

Sometimes you have to be silent to be heard.

Stanislaw J. Lec, Polish writer, 1909–1966

IN TIMES LIKE THE PRESENT, men should utter nothing for which they would not willingly be responsible through time and in eternity.

Abraham Lincoln, U.S. president, 1809–1865 (1862)

THERE'S SOMETHING BETTER THAN SILENCE: it is to speak the truth.

Joseph Kimhi, Spanish poet, 1105–1170

132

ONE ought to be part of the world and also outside it, both involved and detached at the same time.
The Kotzker (Manahem Mendl), Polish clergyman, 1787–1859

The world is won by those who let it go!
Lao-Tzu, Chinese founder of Taoism, sixth century B.C.
(in The Way of Life*)*

The greatest wealth is to live content with little.
Lucretius, Roman poet, first century B.C.

❧

Where there's too much, something is missing.

Yiddish Proverb

❧

Less is more.
Robert Browning, English poet, 1812–1889 (in the poem "Andrea del Sarto" 1855)

134

WHEN WE TRY to pick out anything by itself, we find it hitched to everything else in the universe. One fancies a heart like our own must be beating in every crystal and cell.

John Muir, Scottish-born U.S. naturalist, 1838–1914

ALL SOCIAL AND POLITICAL PROBLEMS ARE INTER-WOVEN. The attempt to deal with neatly defined problems in isolation from one another creates only confusion and disaster.

Alvin Toffler, contemporary U.S. futurist (in The Third Wave, 1980)

Nothing great was ever achieved without enthusiasm.

Samuel Taylor Coleridge, English poet, 1772–1832

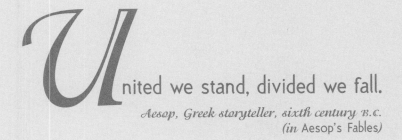

*U*nited we stand, divided we fall.

Aesop, Greek storyteller, sixth century B.C.
(in Aesop's Fables)

IN DIFFICULT AND desperate situations, the boldest plans are safest.

Lucius Marcius, Roman commander, third century B.C.

Nothing ventured, nothing gained.

English Proverb

Many things which cannot be overcome when they are together, yield themselves up when taken little by little.

Sertorius, Roman general and political leader, first century B.C.
(in Plutarch's Lives)

CONCENTRATION is the secret of strength in politics, in war, in trade, in short, in all management of human affairs.

Ralph Waldo Emerson, U.S. philosopher, 1803–1882

The secret of success is constancy of purpose.

Benjamin Disraeli, English prime minister, 1804–1881

We must walk consciously only part way toward our goal, and then leap in the dark to our success.

Henry David Thoreau, U.S. philosopher, 1817–1862

There are some things one can only achieve by a deliberate leap in the opposite direction.

Franz Kafka, Czech writer, 1883–1924

HALF THE FAILURES in life arise from pulling in one's horse as he is leaping.

J. C. Hare (1795–1855) and A. W. Hare (1792–1834), English writers and clergymen

Go back a little to leap the further.

French Proverb

The way out is in.

George Harrison, English songwriter and musician, 1943–2001

The best way out is always through.

Robert Frost, U.S. poet, 1874–1963 (in the poem "A Servant to Servants," 1914)

The longest road is sometimes the quickest way home.

Anonymous

A SMALL LEAK MAY SINK A GREAT SHIP.

English Proverb

The worth of a thing is best known by the want of it.

Scottish Proverb

Nature abhors a vacuum.

Latin Proverb

FORM FOLLOWS FUNCTION.

Louis Henri Sullivan, U.S. architect, 1856–1924

THE implements to him who can handle them.

Napoléon Bonaparte, French general and emperor, 1769–1821

To each circumstance its own law.

Napoléon Bonaparte, French general and emperor, 1769–1821

WOULD YOU PERSUADE, speak of interest, not of reason.

Benjamin Franklin, U.S. printer, inventor, and statesman, 1706–1790 (in Poor Richard's Almanack, 1734)

Don't throw the baby out with the dirty bath water.

German Proverb

No call alligator long mouth till you pass him.

Jamaican Proverb

146

IN the moment of victory, tighten your helmet strap.

Japanese Proverb

If it works, don't fix it.

U.S. Proverb (First Rule of Rural Mechanics)

TRUST BUT VERIFY.

Russian Proverb

Fool me once, shame on you; fool me twice, shame on me.

Proverb

Think globally, but act locally.

René Dubos, French-born U.S. bacteriologist, 1901–1982

FOLLOW your own path, and let people talk.
Dante Alighieri, Italian poet, 1265–1321 (in the poem "Purgatory,"
The Divine Comedy)

When two paths open before you, take the harder one.

Nepalese Proverb (in the film Himalaya, 2001)

LEONARD ROY FRANK, a native of Brooklyn, graduated from the Wharton School of the University of Pennsylvania in 1954. A resident of San Francisco, he managed his own art gallery in the 1970s and has edited a number of books, including *Random House Webster's Quotationary* and *Freedom*. His e-mail address is lfrank@igc.org